NIGHTWALKER

and other poems

Nightwalker

and other poems

Thomas Kinsella

NEW YORK *Alfred · A · Knopf* *1968*

Nightwalker and Other Poems was published in 1967
in slightly different form by The Dolmen Press, Ireland.
Certain of the poems were originally published
by The Dolmen Press in Mr. Kinsella's collections
Downstream (1962) and *Wormwood* (1966) and in the pamphlet
Nightwalker (1967).
Acknowledgment is made to the following publications,
which first printed certain of the poems:
*Arena, Dublin Magazine, Encounter, 15 Poems for
William Shakespeare, The Guardian, Hibernia, Nova, Poetry Ireland,
Programme* for the laying of the foundation stones of
the Belfast New Theatre, *Quarterly Review of Literature,
The Reporter, Shenandoah, Transatlantic Review,
A Tribute for Austin Clarke's 70th Birthday, University Review.*
"Ritual of Departure" and "Mirror in February"
were first published in *Poetry*.

THIS IS A BORZOI BOOK
PUBLISHED BY ALFRED A. KNOPF, INC.

FAIR ELEANOR.   O CHRIST
THEE SAVE.

Contents

I

Our Mother

Tall windows full of sea light,
Two women and a child in tears
Silent among screens and flowers,
The ward a quiet zone of air.

The girl whimpers in bed, remote
Under the anaesthetic still.
She sleeps on her new knowledge, a bride
With bowels burning and disarrayed.

She dreams a red Gorgon-mask
Warped in the steel kidney dish,
The tender offals of her core
Worming around the raw stare.

Her mother watches, struck dumb.
Tears of recognition run
For the stranger, daughter, self, on whom
In fascination her eyes feed,

As mine on her—a revenant,
A rain-worn, delicate
Stone shape that has looked long
Into that other face direct.

In the next bed, dying of age,
The carrier of all our harm
Turns on us an emptiness
Of open mouth and damp eyes.

All three women, two in my care,
The third beyond all care, in tears.
Living, dying, I meet their stare
Everywhere, and cannot move.

Office for the Dead

The grief-chewers enter, their shoes hard on the marble,
In white lace and black skirts, books held to their loins.
A silver pot tosses in its chains as they assemble
About the coffin, heavy under its cloth, and begin.

Back and forth, each side in nasal unison
Against the other, their voices grind across her body.
We watch, kneeling like children, and shrink as their Church
Latin chews our different losses into one

—All but certain images of her pain that will not,
In the coarse process, pass through the cloth and hidden boards
To their peace in the shroud; that delay, still real—

High thin shoulders—eyes boring out of the dusk—
Wistful misshapenness—a stripped, dazzling mouth—
Her frown as she takes the candle pushed into her hands
In the last crisis, propped up, dying with worry.

Sanctus. We listen with bowed heads to the thrash of chains
Measuring the silence. The pot gasps in its smoke.
An animal of metal, dragging itself and breathing . . .

Ballydavid Pier

Noon. The luminous tide
Climbs through the heat, covering
Grey shingle. A film of scum
Searches first among litter,
Cloudy with (I remember)
Life; then crystal-clear shallows
Cool on the stones, silent
With shells and claws, white fish bones;
Farther out a bag of flesh,
Foetus of goat or sheep,
Wavers below the surface.

Allegory forms of itself:
The line of life creeps upward
Replacing one world with another,
The welter of its advance
Sinks down into clarity,
Slowly the more foul
Monsters of loss digest . . .

Small monster of true flesh
Brought forth somewhere
In bloody confusion and error
And flung into bitterness,
Blood washed white:
Does that structure satisfy?

The ghost tissue hangs unresisting
In allegorical waters,
Lost in self-search
—A swollen blind brow
Humbly crumpled over
Budding limbs, unshaken
By the spasms of birth or death.

The Angelus. Faint bell-notes
From some church in the distance
Tremble over the water.
It is nothing. The vacant harbour
Is filling; it will empty.
The misbirth touches the surface
And glistens like quicksilver.

Landscape and Figure

A man stoops low on the overcast plain. He is earthing
Or uprooting among heavy leaves. In the whole field
One dull poppy burns, on the drill by his boots.

The furrows yield themselves to his care. He does not
Lift his head; and would not, though the blight
Breathed on his fields out of the low clouds.

The blight breathes, or does not, invisibly,
As it will. Stalks still break into scattered flower.
Tissue forms about purpose as about seed.

He works toward the fruit of Adam. It darkens the plain,
Its seed a huge brain. The protecting flesh
When it falls will melt away in a kind of mud.

Museum

Out of doors the season dies, a fountain
Ruffles in the wind. The great Museum
Squats closer on its hoard and will not move.
Its blocks of granite, speechless with fatigue,
Imply the slithering pit, the shapelessly-
Adjusting matter of the rubbish heap.

Webs of corridors and numbered rooms
Catch the onward turbulence of forms
Against museum technique; flux disperses
In order everywhere, in glass cases
Or draped or towering in enormous gloom.
Human voice and footstep die.

A dozen tiny coarse clay animals
Picked from a midden—hook-winged geese or hawks,
A bull with pitted head free to move—
Squat blindly. The remote curator speaks:
'In the beginning there were toys, implying love . . .'
Voice and footstep die away.

A Moment's Peace

Summer evening: reclining
Lovers, a pike near the bank,
Stone-still—carnivores,
Ephemerides, touched with gold.
The river surface flows
On in blank passion.

The Serving Maid

She is getting ready in the hall. It is the day for
her weekly visit to her mistress's grave.

Mirror, though you show me my decay
So soon begun—yellowed skin and eyes,
And shadowed lips withering—while I stand
And drag my brush through hair that keeps no shape,
Mirror, mirror, I can laugh at you.
This squawking busybody almost thrives
On jeering at itself; it serves me well.

My eyes (too bright) half question. Too-bright eyes,
I answer with a brighter glitter still.
Doubts harden me. Have I not swallowed back
A hundred frights? Chosen renunciation,
With a hard laugh? Sent heaviness of soul
Bustling out of sight and mind before me?
Chiding cheerily, I rushed to serve

Her soul-consuming ladyship where she lay
Offering helplessness, angrily wasting.
I give God thanks I found her. Such a one . . .
Old feathery bones and flesh to tug and turn
And lift and wipe, jingling the crumpled bed;
Every part, from heels to glistening chin,
A torment of demands. Ignominy-eater!

I come, I come, in decent skirt and jumper
And flat-heeled shoes, with flowers and prayer book
All in order, to remember you;
To kneel by the grave's gravel and pluck the weeds
And replace the withered things—and, if I could,
Grope down at your bones and take away
Even death's eery filth, tidying your substance.

Plot by plot, through shade of stone and yew,
The muddied paths lead to my buried health.
First, your ghostly whispers of complaint:
My face grows pale with wholesome hopelessness.
Then the gasp of self-regard tears happily
And service floods my veins. I give God thanks
I need not sicken of my endless cheer.

Traveller

Behind me my children vanish, left asleep
In their strange bed, in apple-tasted night.
I drive from worry to worry, to where my wife
Struggles for her breath in a private room.

An hour to midnight, and the traps of self
Are open for eighty solitary miles ahead,
In the swerving ditch, in the flash of tree-trunks and hedges.

The brain, woken to itself and restless,
Senses their black mouths muttering in the darkness:
Phrases, echoes of feeling, from other journeys
To bait and confuse the predatory will
And draw it aside, muttering in absent response,
Down stale paths in the dark to a stale lair,
In brainless trance, where it can treadle and chew
Old pangs blunter and smoother, old self-mutilations.

Far ahead on the road the lamps caught something.
A cat. A bird. Mesmerised. It moved,
Eating. It rose slowly, white furred, and flew
Up into the dark. An owl! My heart
Stood still. I had forgotten the very existence . . .

Westland Row

We came to the outer light down a ramp in the dark
Through eddying cold gusts and grit, our ears
Stopped with noise. The hands of the station clock
Stopped, or another day vanished exactly.
The engine departing hammered slowly overhead.
Dust blowing under the bridge, we stooped slightly
With briefcases and books and entered the wind.

The savour of our days restored, dead
On nostril and tongue. Drowned in air,
We stepped on our own traces, not on stone,
Nodded and smiled distantly and followed
Our scattering paths, not stumbling, not touching.

Until, in a breath of benzine from a garage-mouth,
By the Academy of Music coming against us
She stopped an instant in her wrinkled coat
And ducked her childish cheek in the coat-collar
To light a cigarette: seeing nothing,
Thick-lipped, in her grim composure.

Daughterwife, look upon me.

Folk Wisdom

Each year for a short season
The toads stare and wait
And clutch in their being
A shrieking without breath.
There is nothing but the harrow—
Everything speaks its approach;
Even blades of grass,
Flower stems, are harrows' teeth,
Hideous, because they are
Parallel and in earth.

The men are shackling their horses
In the yard. They talk softly
About earth and seed.

Soon the toads will shriek—
Each, as he hears his neighbour,
Gathers all his strength.

And so the curse was lifted,
According to the tale;
One kiss, and a prince stood there
Where a toad had been.
It is possible . . . such a strain,
Under the kiss of the harrow,
Could suffice. As when a man
Clutches his ears, deafened
By his world, to find a jewel
Made of pain in his hands.

Tara

The mist hung on the slope, growing whiter
On the thin grass and dung by the mounds;
It hesitated at the dyke, among briars.

Our children picked up the wrapped flasks, capes and baskets
And we trailed downward among whins and thrones
In a muffled dream, guided by slender axe-shapes.

Our steps scattered on the soft turf, leaving
No trace, the children's voices like light.
Low in the sky behind us, a vast silver shield

Seethed and consumed itself in the thick ether.
A horse appeared at the rampart like a ghost,
And tossed his neck at ease, with a hint of harness.

II

Wormwood

AND A GREAT STAR FELL FROM HEAVEN, BURNING
AS IT WERE A TORCH; AND IT FELL ON THE
THIRD PART OF THE RIVERS AND UPON THE FOUNTAINS
OF WATERS; AND THE NAME OF THE STAR IS
CALLED WORMWOOD; AND THE THIRD PART OF
THE WATERS BECAME WORMWOOD; AND MANY MEN
DIED OF THE WATERS, BECAUSE THEY WERE MADE
BITTER.

Apocalypse 8:10–11

Prologue

Beloved,

    A little of what we have found . . .

    It is certain that maturity and peace are to be sought through ordeal after ordeal, and it seems that the search continues until we fail. We reach out after each new beginning, penetrating our context to know ourselves, and our knowledge increases until we recognise again (more profoundly each time) our pain, indignity and triviality. This bitter cup is offered, heaped with curses, and we must drink or die. And even though we drink we may also die, if every drop of bitterness—that rots the flesh—is not transmuted. (Certainly the individual plight is hideous, each torturing each, but we are guilty, seeing this, to believe that our common plight is only hideous. Believing so, we make it so: pigs in a slaughter-yard that turn and savage each other in a common desperation and disorder.) Death, either way, is guilt and failure. But if we drink the bitterness and can transmute it and continue, we resume in candour and doubt the only individual joy—the restored necessity to learn. Sensing a wider scope, a more penetrating harmony, we begin again in a higher innocence to grow toward the next ordeal.

    Love also, it seems, will continue until we fail: in the sensing of the wider scope, in the growth toward it, in the swallowing and absorption of bitterness, in the resumed innocence . . .

On a Gift in the Shape of a Heart

Open this and you will see
A waste, a nearly naked tree
That will not rest till it is bare,
But shivers, shivers in the air
Scraping at its yellow leaves.
Winter, when the tempest heaves,
It riots in the heaven-sent
Convulsions of self-punishment.

What cannot rest till it is bare,
Though branches crack and fibres tear?

Wormwood

I have dreamt it again: standing suddenly still
In a thicket, among wet trees, stunned, minutely
Shuddering, hearing a wooden echo escape.

A mossy floor, almost colourless, disappears
In depths of rain among the tree shapes.
I am straining, tasting that echo a second longer.

If I can hold it . . . familiar if I can hold it . . .
A black tree with a double trunk—two trees
Grown into one—throws up its blurred branches.

The two trunks in their infinitesimal dance of growth
Have turned completely about one another, their join
A slowly twisted scar, that I recognise . . .

A quick arc flashes sidewise in the air,
A heavy blade in flight. A wooden stroke:
Iron sinks in the gasping core.
                              I will dream it again.

Mask of Love

Mask of Love,
Do you turn to us for peace?
Me, flinching from your stare?
Her, whose face you bear?

Remember how we have climbed
The peaks of stress and stood
Wearily, again
And again, face to face
Across the narrow abyss.

Remember
That our very bodies lack peace:
In tiny darknesses
The skin angrily flames,
Nerve gropes for muscle
Across the silent abyss.

You have seen our nocturnal
Suicidal dance:
She, bent on some tiny mote;
I, doubled in laughter,
Clasping my paunch in grief
For the world in a speck of dust;
Between us, the fuming abyss.

Dumb vapours pour
Where the mask of Love appears,
Reddening, and disappears.

The Secret Garden

The place is growing difficult. Flails of bramble
Crawl into the lawn; on every hand
Glittering, toughened branches drink their dew.
Tiny worlds, drop by drop, tremble
On thorns and leaves; they will melt away.
The silence whispers around us:
Wither, wither, visible, invisible!

A child stands an instant at my knee.
His mouth smells of energy, light as light.
I touch my hand to his pearl flesh, taking strength.
He stands still, absorbing in return
The first taint. Immaculate, the waiting
Kernel of his brain.
How set him free, a son, toward the sour encounter?

Children's voices somewhere call his name.
He runs glittering into the sun, and is gone:
I cultivate my garden for the dew: . . .
A rasping boredom funnels into death!

The sun climbs, a creature of one day,
And the dew dries to dust.

My hand strays out and picks off one sick leaf.

First Light

A prone couple still sleeps.
Light ascends like a pale gas
Out of the sea: dawn-
Light, reaching across the hill
To the dark garden. The grass
Emerges, soaking with grey dew.

Inside, in silence, an empty
Kitchen takes form, tidied and swept,
Blank with marriage—where shrill
Lover and beloved have kept
Another vigil far
Into the night, and raved and wept.

Upstairs a whimper or sigh
Comes from an open bedroom door
And lengthens to an ugly wail
—A child enduring a dream
That grows, at the first touch of day,
Unendurable.

Remembering Old Wars

What clamped us together? When each night fell we lay down
In the smell of decay and slept, our bodies leaking,
Limp as the dead, breathing that smell all night.

Then light prodded us awake, and adversity
Flooded up from inside us as we laboured upright
Once more to face the hells of circumstance.

And so on, without hope of change or peace.
Each dawn, like lovers recollecting their purpose,
We would renew each other with a savage smile.

Je t'adore

The other props are gone.
Sighing in one another's
Iron arms, propped above nothing,
We praise Love the limiter.

The Shoals Returning

In memory of Gerry Flaherty, drowned 1959

I dip the oar and lean
Supported and opposed
On the green flesh of a wave.
The ocean depth swallows
My strength like a stone.

A corpse balanced among
Striped fathoms turns
Over face upward.

He comes from the sea

Down at the gorge-mouth
Slow as a floating stick
A light boat is borne
Into the hall of rock.
It edges to a slope of stone
And washes back and forth,
Treading the watery floor.
Faint strokes of the oars
Echo in the chasm.
A man in cap and boots
Throws his coat onto the slip:
He stoops and flings out
The body of a cod,
A sheaf of slithering mackerel,
A handful of crabs' claws.

✠

He passes on the cliff road
Against depths of marine light:
Narrow-necked, erect,
Averse, in coarse grey jacket
And trousers, wrists loose, his eyes
Black points of spray. A slow
Harsh thunder from below—
The Wave of Tóime snarls
With distance, shudders in its caves;
It writhes milkily,
A ragged foam-web joining
And unlinking among the rocks,
Seizes the cliff in white
Turmoil, sighs and crumbles
—Breakers against breakers—
Chewing the solid earth.

He sings

A voice rises flickering
From palatal darkness, a thin yell
Straining erect, checked
In glottal silence. The song
Articulates and pierces.

A boot scrapes the floor. Live eyes
Shine, each open on its rock,
In horn-darkness of paraffin,
Rope and gas cylinders.
Wet glasses of stout
Cling to boxes and casks;
Men, sunk in shade, listen
On their benches, bodies tainted

With cold sea wind.
Their eyes respond; squat
Entities turn in cranial darkness
In the ravenous element
At the innermost turn of the shell.

He sings at the back of the shop:
Slit eyes above high cheeks, jaws
Drawn back, teeth bared to the voice.
In the exercise of his gift
His throat constricts; speech,
Human proportion, distort
Slightly to permit the cry
That can prepare the spirit
To turn softly and be eaten
In the smell of brine and blood.

Dark shell breath, tatters of mist
And sea-foam blown from the waves
Fly inland. Soiled feathers scatter
On the shingle. Sea birds' fleeting
Bodies pierce the wind.

He returns

In that Autumn, after fifteen
Years, a new direction
Loosened the seed in the depths;
The mackerel shoals reappeared
And the water in the Sound shivered.

The boats waited at Smerwyck,
Black-skinned, crook-backed,

On the grass by the drying boat-slip;
The rocky knife-sharp shore
Drained bare: crayfish stared:
Brutal torso of conger
Slid through a choked slit—
Naked savagery
On which, when the eyes lift,
An infinite sheen alights,
A sheet of blinding water
Pierced by black points of rock.
By nightfall the bay ran cold
With the distant returning tide
Under the wall of Mount Brandon.
The clefts brimmed in darkness.

✠

Booted spirits are at work;
A heavy step scrapes
On the slip; a boat tosses
With a feathery splash. They vanish
Over covered razors of rock
And move out with crisp
Tangles of net, vague
Oar-voices, a fading
Taint of canvas and rope,
Past cliff wall and washed rocks
Over meshes of hissing foam.
They cross into the Sound
And climb the swell blindly,
Dropping in dark valleys.

Nets are shaken out
And swallowed into the sea.
The lines reach far down
And open everywhere
Among the haunted levels.
A million shadows
Pursue their staring will
Along echoing cold paths.
The delicate veil of garrottes
Drags, scarcely breathing,
Then touches a living shoal.
Fierce bodies leap into being
Strangling all over the net,
An anguish of shivering lives.
They gather weight, shudder
By shudder, and—gazing about them—
Turn to unbearable stone.

He disappears

Dawn opened on a jewel
Twisting in the sea
Under the empty boat
—A net of suffocated fish
Tied fast to the seat board
Pulling the head down in the waves:
Two thousand mackerel
Torn from the intense shoal,
Stopped dead and gathered up
With mourning devils' mouths
And scales and rigid eyes
In a cluster shaped by its own
Weight against the diamond-

37

Meshes of its bonds.
The drowned men have fallen away
Through the water and separated
With slow hair in the calm.
Now their jewel drifts
—Until it rots to pieces—
For anyone to find.

✠

A withered man, a coat
Across his shoulders, watches
From the cliff over the gorge
—A black outcrop thrust
Partly out of the soil
Into the salt wind.
The shale-grass shivers around him.
He turns a shrunken mask
Of cheekbone and jawbone
And pursed ancient mouth
On the sea surface.
A windswept glitter of light
Murmurs toward the land.
His eyes, out of tortoise lids,
Assess the crystalline plasm,
Formations of water
Under falls of air.

III

Before Sleep

It is time for bed. The cups and saucers are gathered
And stacked in the kitchen, the tray settled
With your tablets, a glass, a small jug of orange.
Are the windows shut, and all the doors locked?

I pass near the desk in my room and stand a minute
Looking down the notes I made this morning.
Yes: tomorrow it might do to begin . . .
Thunder whispers far-off among my papers.

The wall opposite is blank but alive
—Standing water over sunken currents.
The currents pursue their slow eddies through the house
Scarcely loosening as yet the objects of our love.

Soon the Falls will thunder, our love's detritus
Slide across the brim seriatim, glittering,
And vanish, swallowed into that insane
White roar. Chaos. All battered, scattered.

Yes: in the morning I will put on the cataract,
Give it veins, clutching hands, the short shriek of thought.

Magnanimity

(for Austin Clarke's seventieth birthday)

So I forgot
His enmity."
Green abundance
Last summer in Coole Park. A stone hearth
Surviving; a grassy path by the orchard wall.

You stared through chicken-wire at the initials
Cut in Lady Gregory's tree, scars grown thick.
Overhead a breath passed magniloquently through the leaves,

Branches swayed and sank. You turned away and said
Coole might be built again as a place for poets.
Through the forbidden tree magnanimity passed.

I am sure that there are no places for poets,
Only changing habitations for verse to outlast.
Your own house, isolated by a stream, exists

For your use while you live—like your body and your world.
Helpless commonness encroaches, chews the soil,
Squats ignobly. Within, consciousness intensifies:

Sharp small evils magnify into Evil,
Pity and mockery suggest some idea of Good,
Fright stands up stiffly under pain of death.

Houses shall pass away, and all give place
To signposts and chicken-wire.
                              A tree stands.
Pale cress persists on a shaded stream.

The Poet Egan O'Rahilly,
Homesick in Old Age

He climbed to his feet in the cold light, and began
The decrepit progress again, blown along the cliff road,
Bent with curses above the shrew his stomach.

The salt abyss poured through him, more raw
With every laboured, stony crash of the waves:
His teeth bared at their voices, that incessant dying.

Iris leaves bent on the ditch, unbent,
Shivering in the wind: leaf-like spirits
Chattered at his death-mark as he passed.

He pressed red eyelids: aliens crawled
Breaking princely houses in their jaws;
Their metal faces reared up, chewing at light.

"Princes overseas, who slipped away
In your extremity, no matter where I travel
I find your great houses like stopped hearts.

Likewise your starving children—though I nourish
Their spirit, and my own, on the lists of praises
I make for you still in the cooling den of my craft.

Our enemies multiply. They have recruited the sea:
Last night, the West's rhythmless waves destroyed my sleep;
This morning, winkle and dogfish persisting in the stomach . . ."

"To Autumn"

Insect beads crawl on the warm soil,
Black carapaces; brittle harvest spiders
Clamber weightlessly among dry roots
In soundless bedlam. He sits still writing
At the edge of the wheatfield, a phantasm of flesh
                    while thy hook
        Spares . . .
Ripened leagues, a plain of odorous seed,
Quiet scope, season of mastery,
The last of peace. Along ethereal summits,
A gleam of disintegrating materials
Held a frail instant at unearthly heights.

Death in Ilium

(In Yeats's centenary year)

Attention and power relax,
Truth deserts the body:
Hector among his books
Drops dead in the dust.

The tireless shadow-eaters
Close in with tough nose
And pale fang to expose
Fibre, weak flesh, speech organs.

They eat, but cannot eat.
Dog-faces in his bowels,
Bitches at his face,
He grows whole and remote.

Soft Toy

I am soiled with the repetition of your loves and hatreds
    And other experiments. You do not hate me,
Crumpled in my corner. You do not love me,
    A small heaped corpse. My face of beaten fur
Responds as you please: if you do not smile
    It does not smile; to impatience or distaste
It answers blankness, beyond your goodwill
    —Blank conviction, beyond your understanding or mine.

I lie limp with use and re-use, listening.
    Loose ends of conversations, hesitations,
Half-beginnings that peter out in my presence,
    Are enough. I understand, with a flame of shame
Or a click of ease or joy, inert. Knowledge
    Into resignation: the process drives deeper,
Grows clearer, eradicating chance growths of desire
    —And colder: all possibilities of desire.

My button-brown hard eyes fix on your need
    To grow, as you crush me with tears and throw me aside.
Most they reflect, but something absorb—brightening
    In response, with energy, to the energy of your changes.
Clutched tightly through the night, held before you,
    Ragged and quietly crumpled, as you thrust, are thrust,
In dull terror into your opening brain,
    I face the dark with eyes that cannot close

—The cold, outermost points of your will, as you sleep.
    Between your tyrannous pressure and the black
Resistance of the void my blankness hardens
    To a blunt probe, a cold pitted grey face.

Leaf-Eater

On a shrub in the heart of the garden,
On an outer leaf, a grub twists
Half its body, a tendril,
This way and that in blind
Space: no leaf or twig
Anywhere in reach; then gropes
Back on itself and begins
To eat its own leaf.

IV

Nightwalker

THE GREATER PART MUST BE CONTENT TO BE AS
THOUGH THEY HAD NOT BEEN.

Mindful of the
shambles of the day
But mindful, under the
blood's drowsy humming,
Of will that gropes for
structure—nonetheless
Not unmindful of
the madness without,
The madness within (the
book of reason slammed
Open, slammed shut)
we presume to say:

I

I only know things seem and are not good.

A brain in the dark, and bones, out exercising
Shadowy flesh; fitness for the soft belly,
Fresh air for lungs that take no pleasure any longer.
The smell of gardens under suburban lamplight,
Clipped privet, a wall blotted with shadows
—Monsters of ivy squat in lunar glare.
                    There, above the roofs,
It hangs, like a fat skull, or the pearl knob
Of a pendulum at the outermost reach of its swing,
Motionless. It is about to detach
Its hold on the upper night, for the return.
                    Aye, I remember talk of it,
Though only a child. Not far from here it passed through
                    remorseless cratered face
Swift as the wind: a bludgeon tears free
From the world's bones, spikes breaking off
—Millions of little sharp limbs, jets of blood
Petrified in terror, jetted screams—
Then plunges upward far into the darkness—
                    It meant little to me then,
Though I remember playing in the silence
When the rain of fragments dropped in the streets afterward
—Bone-splinters, silvery slivers of screams,
Blood-splinters rattling, like crimson flint.
                    There it hangs,
A mask of grey dismay sagging open
In the depths of torture, moron voiceless moon.
That dark area, the mark of Cain.

55

My shadow twists about my feet in the light
Of every passing street-lamp. Will-o'-the-wisp
In a bay window; a shadow slumped in the corner
Of a living-room, in blue trance, buried
Alive, two blank eyes. On a tiny screen
Mouths open and shut, and bodies move
Obliquely and stoop, flickering—

       embalmers
In eery light underground; their arms
Toil in silence.

   A laboratory
Near Necropolis. It is midnight.
A shade enters,

     patrolling the hive of his brain.

       Window after window,
The same unearthly light consumes pitilessly.
Surely we can never die, sick spirits . . .

      The minions stretch at rest,
Pale entities wound in a drowsy humming
At the brink of sleep. They snuggle in their cells
Faintly luminous, like grubs—abdominal
Body-juices and paper-thin shells, in their thousands,
In the smashable wax, o moon!

      Musing thus,
I stroll upon my way, a vagabond
Tethered. My shadow twists at their feet.

I must lie down with them all soon and sleep,
And rise with them again when the new dawn
Has touched our pillows and our wet pallor
And roused us. We'll come scratching in our waistcoats
Down to the kitchen for a cup of tea;
Then with our briefcases, through wind or rain,
Past our neighbours' gardens—Melrose, Bloomfield—
To wait at the station, fluttering our papers,
Assembled for the day's toil, palping the cool wind.
                              Is it not right to serve
Our banks and businesses and government
As together we develop our community
On clear principles, with no fixed ideas?
And (twitching our thin umbrellas) acceptable
That during a transitional period
Development should express itself in forms
Without principle, based on fixed ideas . . .
                              Robed in spattered iron
At the harbour mouth she stands, Productive Investment,
And beckons the nations through our gold half-door:
Lend me your wealth, your cunning and your drive,
Your arrogant refuse;
                         let my people serve them
Bottled fury in our new hotels,
While native businessmen and managers
Drift with them, chatting, over to the window
To show them our growing city, give them a feeling
Of what is possible; our labour pool,
The tax concessions to foreign capital,
How to get a nice estate though German,
Even collect some of our better young artists.

                              Morose condemnation . . .
It is a weakness, and turns on itself.
                                        Clean bricks
Are made of mud; we need them for our tower.

                        ✠

Spirit-skeletons are straggling into view
From the day's depths. You can pick them out
In the night sky, with a little patience:
                              Pale influences . . .
The wakeful Twins,
                        Bruder und Schwester
—Two young Germans I had in this morning
Wanting to transfer investment income;
The sister a business figurehead, her brother
Otterfaced, with exasperated smiles
Assuming—pressing until he achieved—response.
Handclasp; I do not exist; I cannot take
My eyes from their pallor. A red glare
Plays on their faces, livid with little splashes
Of blazing fat. The oven door closes.
                              All about and above me
The officials on the corridors or in their rooms
Work, or overwork, with mixed motives
Or none. We dwell together in urgency;
Dominate, entering middle age; subserve,
Aborting vague tendencies with buttery smiles.
Among us, behind locked doors, the ministers
Are working, with a sureness of touch found early,

In the nation's birth—the blood of enemies
And brothers dried on their hide long ago.
Dragon old men, upright and stately and blind,
Or shuffling in the corridor finding a key,
Their youth cannot die in them; it will be found
Beating with violence when their bodies rot.
                              What occupies them
As they sit in their rooms? What they already are?
Shadow-flesh . . . claimed by pattern still living,
Linked into constellations with their dead . . .
                              Look! The Wedding Group:
The Groom, the Best Man, the Fox, and their three ladies
—A tragic tale: soon, the story tells,
Enmity sprang up between them, and the Fox
Took to the wilds. Then, to the Groom's sorrow,
His dear friend left him also, vowing hatred.
So they began destroying the Groom's substance
And he sent out to hunt the Fox, but trapped
His friend instead; mourning, he slaughtered him.
Shortly, in his turn, the Groom was savaged
On a Sunday morning, no one knows by whom
(Though it's known the Fox is a friend of Death and rues
Nothing).
                    Over here, in the same quarter,
The Two Executioners—Groom and Weasel—
'77' burning into each brow;
And look, the vivid Weasel there again,
Dancing crookbacked under the Player King
—A tragicomical tale:
                              how the Fox, long after,
Found a golden instrument one day,

A great complex gold horn, left at his door;
He examined it with little curiosity,
Wanting no gold or music; observed the mouthpiece,
Impossible to play with fox's lips,
And gave it with dull humour to his old enemy
The Weasel—who recognised the horn
Of the Player King, and bared his needle teeth.
He took it, hammered on it with a stick
And pranced about in blithe pantomime,
His head cocked to enjoy the golden clouts,
While the Fox from time to time nodded his mask.

II

The human taste grows faint.
                    It is gone,
Leaving a taste of self and laurel leaves
                and rotted salt:
The gardens begin to smell of soaked sand
And half-stripped rocks in the dark. My bones obey
The sighing of the tide.
              Another turning:
A cast-iron lamp-standard sheds yellow light
On the sea-wall; other lamps are lighting
Along a terrace of Victorian red brick.
Not a breath of wind. Joyce's Martello tower
Rises into the dark near the Forty Foot
On a prow frozen to stone.
              Crossing the road
I hear my footsteps echo back from the terrace.
              A sheet of newspaper

Gleams yellowish in the gutter. The morning *TIMES:*
Our new young minister glares from a photograph
—On horseback, in hunting pinks, from a low angle,
Haunch on haunch. Snigger, and by God . . .
Big snails glisten among roots of iris.
                    The tide is drawing back
From the promenade, far as the lamplight can reach,
Trickling under the weed, into night's cave.
                    Note the silence.
Light never strays there. Nothing has a shadow there.
When a wind blows there . . .
                    A rustle in the gutter:
The hair stirs! Stealing over the waters,
Through the smell of seaweed, a spectral stink of horse
And rider's sweat . . .
                    What's that, outside the light?

✠

Watcher in the tower, be with me now
At your parapet, above the glare of the lamps.
Turn your milky spectacles on the sea
Unblinking; cock your ear.
                    A rich darkness
Alive with signals: lights flash and wink;
Little bells clonk in the channel near the rocks;
Howth twinkles across the bay; ship-lights move
By invisible sea-lanes; the Baily light
Flickers, as it sweeps the middle darkness,
On some commotion . . .

A dripping cylinder
Big as a ship's funnel, pokes into sight,
Picked out by the moon. Two blazing eyes.
Then a whole head. Shoulders of shadowy muscle
Lit from within by joints and bones of light.
Another head . . . animal, with nostrils straining
Open, red as embers; goggle-eyes.
A spectral whinny! Forehoofs scrape at the night,
A rider grunts and urges.
                          Father of Authors!
It is himself! In silk hat and jowls,
Accoutred in stern jodhpurs! The sonhusband
Coming in his power: mounting to glory
On his big white harse
                        climbing the dark
To his mansion in the sky, to take his place
In the influential circle—a new sign:
                          Foxhunter.
                                  Subjects will find
The going hard but rewarding. You may give offence
But this should pass. Marry the Boss's daughter.

The newspaper settles down in the gutter again:
                THE ARCHBISHOP ON MARRIAGE
NEW MOVES TO RESTORE THE LANGUAGE
                          THE NEW IRELAND . . .
              still awkward in the saddle
But able and willing for the foul ditch.
You'll sit as well as any at the kill,
Dark brother. What matter what iron Fausts
Open the gates?

It is begun: the curs
Mill and yelp at your heel, backsnapping and grinning.
They eye your back. Watch the smile of the dog.
They wait your signal, the kick of dirt in the teeth,
To turn them, in the old miracle,
To a pack of lickspittles, running as one.

✠

The foot of the tower. An angle where the darkness
Is complete. The parapet is empty.
A backdrop of constellations, crudely done
And mainly unfamiliar; they are arranged
To suggest a chart of the brain. Music far off.
In the part of the little harbour that can be seen
The moon is reflected in low water.
Beyond, the lamps on the terrace.
                              The music fades.
                    Snuggle into the skull.
Total darkness wanders among my bones.
Lung-tips flutter. Wavelets lap the shingle.
From the vest's darkness, smell of my body:
                    Chalk dust and flowers . . .
Faint brutality. Shoes creak in peace.
Brother Burke flattens his soutane
Against the desk:
                    but the authorities
Used the National Schools to try to conquer
The Irish national spirit, at the same time
Exterminating what they called our 'jargon'

—The Irish language; in which Saint Patrick, Saint Bridget
And Saint Columcille taught and prayed!
Edmund Ignatius Rice founded our Order
To provide schools that were national in more than name.
Pupils from our schools played their part,
As you know, in the fight for freedom. And you will be called
In your different ways—to work for the native language,
To show your love by working for your country.
Today there are Christian Brothers' boys
Everywhere in the Government—the present Taoiseach
Sat where one of you is sitting now.
It wasn't long before Her Majesty
Gave us the Famine—the Starvation, as Bernard Shaw,
A godless writer, called it more accurately.
                              A hand is laid on my brow.
A voice breathes: You will ask are we struck dumb
By the unsimplifiable. Take these . . .
Bread of certainty; scalding soup of memories,
For my drowsy famine—martyrs in a dish
Of scalding tears: food of dragon men
And my own dragon half. Fierce pity!
                              The Blessed Virgin smiles
From her waxed pedestal, like young Victoria;
A green snake wriggles under her heel
Beside a vase of tulips.
                              Adolescents,
Celibates, we offer up our vows
To God and Ireland in Her name, grateful
That by our studies here they may not lack
Civil servants in a state of grace.
                              The tall partition rattles

In the draught. Rain against the windows.
A shiver clothes the flesh
                        bittersweet.
                         A seamew passes over,
Whingeing:
              Eire, Eire . . . is there none
To hear? Is all lost?
                  Not yet all; a while still
Your voice . . .
              Alas, I think I will dash myself
At the stones. I will become a wind on the sea
Or a wave of the sea again, or a sea sound.
At the first light of the sun I stirred on my rock;
I have seen the sun go down at the end of the world;
Now I fly across the face of the moon.
                 A dying language echoes
Across a century's silence.
                    It is time,
Lost soul, I turned for home.
                   Sad music steals
Over the scene.
             Hesitant, cogitating, exit.

III

Home and beauty.
                Her dear shadow on the blind,
The breadknife . . . She was slicing and buttering
A loaf of bread. My heart stopped. I starved for speech.
I believe now that love is half persistence,
A medium in which, from change to change,

65

Understanding may be gathered.
                              The return:
                              Virgin most pure, bright
In the dregs of the harbour: moon of my dismay,
Quiet as oil, enormous in her shaggy pool.
Her brightness, reflected on earth, in heaven,
Consumes my sight. Gradually, as my brain
At a great distance swims in the steady light,
Scattered notes, scraps of newspaper, photographs,
Begin to flow unevenly toward the pool
And gather into a book before her stare.
Her mask darkens as she reads, to my faint terror,
But she soon brightens a little, and smiles wanly:
                              It was a terrible time,
Nothing but sadness and horrors of one kind and another.
I came to take the waters. The sun shone brightly,
Which was very pleasant, and made it less gloomy,
Though my tears flowed again and again. When I drank
I felt all my patience and trust coming back.
From time to time it seems that everything
Is breaking down; but we must never despair.
There are times it is all a meaningful drama
Beginning in the grey mists of antiquity
And reaching through the years to unknown goals
In the consciousness of man, which is very soothing.
                              A wind sighs. The pool
Shivers: the tide at the turn. Odour of lamplight,
Sour soil, the sea bed, passes like a ghost
—The hem of her invisible garment.
                              Our mother
Rules on high, queenlike, pale with control.

66

Hatcher of peoples!
Incline from your darkness into mine!
I stand at the ocean's edge, my head fallen back
Heavy with your control, and oppressed!

✠

That mad stare—the pulse hisses in my ear—
I am an arrow piercing the void, unevenly
As I correct and correct, but swift as thought.
I arrive, enveloped in blinding silence.
                                        No wind stirs
On the dust floor. Far as the eye can see
Rock needles stand up from the plain; the horizon
A ring of sharp mountains like broken spikes.
Hard bluish light beats down, to kill
Any bodily thing—but a million dead voices hide
From it in the dust, without hope of peace.
(A cloud bursts from the ground, rock fragments scatter
In total silence.) A true desert, naked
To every peril. The shadows are alive:
They scuttle and flicker among the rock needles,
Squat and suck the dry juice, inspect
The eggs of shadow beneath the surface, twitching
Madly in their cells.
                        The earth, at the full,
Hangs in blue splendour in the sky.
                                    I believe I have heard
Of this place.
                In the mind darkness tosses:

The light deceives. A vivid ghost sea
Quivers and dazzles for miles.
                              Let us take the waters.
Stoop down, run the fingers along the brink.
It has a human taste, but sterile; odourless.
Massed human wills . . .
                              A dust plain flickering . . .
I think this is the Sea of Disappointment.

Ritual of Departure

A man at the moment of departure, turning
To leave, treasures some stick of furniture
With slowly blazing eyes, or the very door
Broodingly with his hand as it falls shut.

✠

Open the soft string that clasps in series
A dozen silver spoons, and spread them out,
Matched perfectly, one maker and to the year:
                              brilliance in use that fell
Open before the first inheritor.

A stag crest stares from the soft solid silver
And grimaces, with fat cud-lips but jaws
That could crack bones.
                            The stag heart stumbles.
He rears at bay, slavering silver; rattles
A trophied head among my gothic rocks.

✠

Stones of a century and a half ago.
The same city distinct in the same air,
More open in an earlier evening light.
Dublin under the Georges . . .
                              stripped of Parliament,

69

Lying powerless in sweet-breathing death-ease
                              after forced Union.
Under a theatre of swift-moving cloud
Domes, pillared, in the afterglow—
A portico, beggars moving on the steps—
A horserider locked in soundless greeting,
Bowed among dogs and dung; the panelled vista
Closing on pleasant smoke-blue far-off hills.

                    ✠

The ground opens. Pale wet potatoes
Break into light. The black soil falls from their flesh,
From the hands that tear them up and spread them out
In fresh disorder, perishable roots to eat.
                              The fields vanish in rain
Among white rock and red bog—saturated
High places traversed by spring sleet
Or thrust up in summer through the thin wind
Into pounding silence. Farther south: cattle,
Wheat, salmon glistening, the sea.
Landscape with ancestral figures . . . names
Settling and intermixing on the earth,
The seed in slow retreat, through time and blood,
Into bestial silence.
                              Faces sharpen and grow blank,
With eyes for nothing.
                              And their children's children
Venturing to disperse, some came to Dublin
To vanish in the city lanes.
                              I saw the light

Enter from the laneway, through the scullery
To the foot of the stairs, creep across grey floorboards,
Sink in plush in the staleness of an inner room.

I scoop at the earth, and sense famine, a first
Sourness in the clay. The roots tear softly.

Phoenix Park

THE PHÆNIX BUILDS THE PHÆNIX'S NEST,
LOVE'S ARCHITECTURE IS HIS OWN

I

One stays or leaves. The one who returns is not
The one, etcetera. And we are leaving.
You are quiet and watchful, this last visit.
We pass the shapes of cattle blurred by moisture;
A few deer lift up their wet horns from the grass;

A smoke-soft odour of graves . . . our native damp.
A twig with two damp leaves drops on the bonnet
From the upper world, trembling; shows us its clean
Fracture and vanishes, snatched off by the wind:
Droplets of moisture shudder on the windscreen.

—You start at the suddenness, as though it were
Your own delicate distinct flesh that had snapped.
What was in your thoughts . . . saying after a while
I write you nothing, no love songs, any more?
Fragility echoing fragilities . . .

The Chapelizod Gate. Dense trees on our right,
Sycamores and chestnuts around the entrance
To St. Mary's Hospital. Under their shade
I entered long ago, took the twisting paths
To find you by the way of hesitation.

You lay still, brilliant with illness, behind glass;
I stooped and tasted your life until you woke
And your body's fever leaped out at my mind.
There's a fever now that eats everything
—Everything but the one positive dream.

That dream . . . it is something I might offer you,
Sorry it is not anything for singing;
Your body would know that it is positive
—Everything you know you know bodily.
And the preparation also . . . Take them both.

The preparation Near a rounded wooded hillock, where a stream
Drains under the road, inside Islandbridge Gate,
A child stooped to the grass, picking and peeling
And devouring mushrooms straight out of the
      ground:
Death-pallor in their dry flesh, the taste of death.

Later, in freezing darkness, I came alone
To the railings round the Pond, whispered *Take me,
I am nothing.* But the words hovered, their sense
Revealing opposite within opposite.
Understanding moved, a silent bright discus.

As, when I walked this glimmering road, it did
Once, between night-trees. The stars seemed in my
      grasp,
Changing places among the naked branches
—Thoughts drawing into order under night's skull.
But something moved on the path: faint, sweet
      breathing—

A woman stood, thin and tired, in a light dress,
And interrupted kindly, in vague hunger.
Her hand rested for a moment on my sleeve.
I studied her and saw shame does not matter,
Nor kindness when there's no answering hunger,

And passed by; her eyes burned . . . So equipped to
     learn
I found you, in feverish sleep, where you lay.
Midsummer, and I had tasted your knowledge,
My flesh blazing in yours; Autumn, I had learned
Giving without tearing is not possible.

✠

The Furry Glen: grass sloping down to the lake,
Where she stooped in her Communion finery,
Our first-born, Sara in innocence, and plucked
Something out of the ground for us to admire.
The child smiled in her white veil, self-regarding.

II

We leave the Park through Knockmaroon Gate and
     turn,
Remembering, downhill to the Liffey Road
With the ache of dampness growing in our lungs.
Along river curves sunk under heavy scenes,
By the Strawberry Beds, under gravel slopes,

To sit drinking in a back bar in Lucan
At a glass table, under a staring light,
Talking of departure. You are uneasy;
I make signs on the surface with my wet glass
In human regret, but human certainty:

Whatever the ultimate grotesqueries
They'll have to root in more than this sour present.
The ordeal-cup, set at each turn, so far
We have welcomed, sour or sweet. What matter
    where
It waits next for us, if we will take and drink?

The dream Look into the cup: the tissues of order
Form under your stare. The living surfaces
Mirror each other, gather everything
Into their crystalline world. Figure echoes
Figure faintly in the saturated depths;

Revealed by faint flashes of each other
They light the whole confines: a fitful garden . . .
A child plucks death and tastes it; a shade watches
Over him; the child fades and the shade, made flesh,
Stumbles on understanding, begins to fade,

Bequeathing a child in turn; women-shapes pass
Unseeing, full of knowledge, through each other
. . . All gathered. And the crystal so increases,
Eliciting in its substance from the dark
The slowly forming laws it increases by,

Laws of order I find I have discovered
Mainly at your hands . . . of failure and increase,
The stagger and recovery of spirit:
That life is hunger, hunger is for order,
And hunger satisfied brings on new hunger

Till there's nothing to come; —let the crystal crack
On some insoluble matter, then its heart
Shudders and accepts the flaw, adjusts on it
Taking new strength—given the positive dream.
Given, with your permission, undying love . . .

That while the dream lasts there's a total hunger
That gropes out disappearing just past touch,
A blind human face burrowing in the void,
Eating new tissue down into existence
Until every phantasm—all that can come—

Has roamed in flesh and vanished, or passed inward
Among the echoing figures to its place,
And this live world is emptied of its hunger
While the crystal world, undying, crowds with light,
Filling the cup . . . That there is one last phantasm

Who'll come painfully in old lewd nakedness
—Loose needles of bone coming out through his
        fat—
Groping with an opposite, equal hunger,
Thrusting a blind skull from its tatters of skin
As from a cowl, to smile in understanding

And total longing; aching to plant one kiss
In the live crystal as it aches with fullness,
And accommodate his body with that kiss;
But that forever he will pause, the final
Kiss ungiveable. Giving without tearing

Is not possible; to give totality
Is to be torn totally, a nothingness
Reaching out in stasis a pure nothingness.
—Therefore everlasting life, the unmoving
Stare of full desire. Given undying love . . .

✠

I give them back not as your body knows them
—That flesh is finite, so in love we persist;
That love is to clasp simply, question fiercely;
That getting life we eat pain in each other—
But mental, in my fever—mere idea.

III

We finish, our glasses drained, and rise to go,
And stand again in the saturated air
Near the centre of the village, breathing in
Faint smells of chocolate and beer, fallen leaves
In the gutter, blank autumnal essences.

You wait a minute on the path, absently
—Against massed brown trees—tying a flimsy scarf
At your neck. Fair Ellinor. O Christ thee save.
And I taste a structure, ramshackle, ghostly,
Vanishing on my tongue, given and taken,

Distinct. A ghost of that ghost persists, structure
Without substance, all about us, in the air,
Among the trees, before us at the crossroads,
On the stone bridge, insinuating itself
Into being. Undying . . . And I shiver

Seeing your thoughtless delicate completeness.
Love, it is certain, continues till we fail,
Whenever (with your forgiveness) that may be
—At any time, now, totally, ordeal
Succeeding ordeal till we find some death,

Hoarding bitterness, or refusing the cup;
Then the vivifying eye clouds, and the thin
Mathematic tissues loosen, and the cup
Thickens, and order dulls and dies in love's death
And melts away in a hungerless no dream.

✠

Fragility echoing fragilities
From whom I have had every distinctness
Accommodate me still, where—folded in peace
And undergoing with ghostly gaiety
Inner immolation, shallowly breathing—

You approach the centre by its own sweet light.
I consign my designing will stonily
To your flames. Wrapped in that rosy fleece, two lives
Burn down around one love, one flickering-eyed
Stone self becomes more patient than its own stone.

✠

The road divides and we can take either way,
Etcetera. The Phoenix Park; Inchicore,
Passing Phoenix Street . . . the ways are one, sweet
　　choise,
Our selves become our own best sacrifice.
Continue, so. We'll perish in each other.

IV

The tires are singing, cornering back and forth
In our green world again; into groves of trees,
By lake and open park, past the hospital.
The west ignites behind us; round one more turn
Pale light in the east hangs over the city:

An eighteenth century prospect to the sea—
River haze; gulls; spires glitter in the distance
Above faint multitudes. Barely audible
A murmur of soft, wicked laughter rises.
Dublin, the umpteenth city of confusion . . .

A theatre for the quick articulate,
The agonized genteel, their artful watchers . . .
Malice as entertainment. Asinine feast
Of sowthistles and brambles! And there dead men,
Half hindered by dead men, tear down dead beauty.

Return by the mental ways we have ourselves
Established, past visages of memory
Set at every turn: where we smiled and passed
Without a second thought, or stood in the rain
And whispered bitterly; where we roamed at night

Drunk in joyful love, looking for enemies
(They in our bodies—white handkerchief, white
        page,
Crimsoned with panic); where naked by firelight
We stood and rested from each other and took
Our burden from the future, eyes crystalline,

My past alive in you, a gift of tissue
Torn free from my life in an odour of books.
That room . . . The shapes of tiredness had
        assembled
Long ago in its four dark corners, before
You came, waiting, while you were everywhere.

One midnight at the starlit sill I let them
Draw near. Loneliness drew into order:
A thought of fires in the hearts of darknesses,
A darkness at the heart of every fire,
Darkness, fire, darkness, threaded on each other—

The orders of stars fixed in abstract darkness,
Darknesses of worlds sheltering in their light;
World darkness harbouring orders of cities
Whose light at midnight harbours human darkness;
The human dark pierced by solitary fires . . .

Such fires as one I have seen gutter and fail
And, as it sank, reveal the fault in its heart
Opening on abstract darkness, where hunger
Came with gaping kiss over terrible wastes
—Till the flames sprang up and blindness was
      restored.

Attracted from the night by my wakefulness
Certain half-dissolved—half-formed—beings
      loomed close:
A child with eaten features eating something—
Another, with unfinished features, in white—
They hold hands. A shadow bends to protect them.

The shadow tries to speak, but its tongue stumbles.
A snake out of the void moves in my mouth, sucks
At triple darkness. A few ancient faces
Detach and begin to circle. Deeper still
Delicate distinct tissue begins to form.

V

from DOWNSTREAM
(1962)

Mirror in February

The day dawns with scent of must and rain,
Of opened soil, dark trees, dry bedroom air.
Under the fading lamp, half dressed—my brain
Idling on some compulsive fantasy—
I towel my shaven lip and stop, and stare,
Riveted by a dark exhausted eye,
A dry downturning mouth.

It seems again that it is time to learn,
In this untiring, crumbling place of growth
To which, for the time being, I return.
Now plainly in the mirror of my soul
I read that I have looked my last on youth
And little more; for they are not made whole
That reach the age of Christ.

Below my window the awakening trees,
Hacked clean for better bearing, stand defaced
Suffering their brute necessities,
And how should the flesh not quail that span for span
Is mutilated more? In slow distaste
I fold my towel with what grace I can,
Not young and not renewable, but man.

Chrysalides

Our last free summer we mooned about at odd hours
Pedalling slowly through country towns, stopping to eat
Chocolate and fruit, tracing our vagaries on the map.

At night we watched in the barn, to the lurch of melodeon
    music,
The crunching boots of countrymen—huge and weightless
As their shadows—twirling and leaping over the yellow
    concrete.

Sleeping too little or too much, we awoke at noon
And were received with womanly mockery into the kitchen,
Like calves poking our faces in with enormous hunger.

Daily we strapped our saddlebags and went to experience
A tolerance we shall never know again, confusing
For the last time, for example, the licit and the familiar.

Our instincts blurred with change; a strange wakefulness
Sapped our energies and dulled our slow-beating hearts
To the extremes of feeling—insensitive alike

To the unique succession of our youthful midnights,
When by a window ablaze softly with the virgin moon
Dry scones and jugs of milk awaited us in the dark,

Or to lasting horror: a wedding flight of ants
Spawning to its death, a mute perspiration
Glistening like drops of copper, agonised, in our path.

Dick King

In your ghost, Dick King, in your phantom vowels I read
That death roves our memories igniting
Love. Kind plague, low voice in a stubbled throat,
You haunt with the taint of age and of vanished good,
Fouling my thought with losses.

Clearly now I remember rain on the cobbles,
Ripples in the iron trough, and the horses' dipped
Faces under the Fountain in James's Street,
When I sheltered my nine years against your buttons
And your own dread years were to come;

And your voice, in a pause of softness, named the dead,
Hushed as though the city had died by fire,
Bemused . . . discovering, discovering
A gate to enter temperate ghosthood by;
And I squeezed your fingers till you found again
My hand hidden in yours.
                        I squeeze your fingers:

      Dick King was an upright man.
      Sixty years he trod
      The dull stations underfoot.
      Fifteen he lies with God.

      By the salt seaboard he grew up
      But left its rock and rain
      To bring a dying language east
      And dwell in Basin Lane.

By the Southern Railway he increased:
His second soul was born
In the clangour of the iron sheds,
The hush of the late horn.

An invalid he took to wife.
She prayed her life away;
Her whisper filled the whitewashed yard
Until her dying day.

And season in, season out,
He made his wintry bed.
He took the path to the turnstile
Morning and night till he was dead.

He clasped his hands in a Union ward
To hear St. James's bell.
I searched his eyes though I was young,
The last to wish him well.

A Country Walk

Sick of the piercing company of women
I swung the gate shut with a furious sigh,
Rammed trembling hands in pockets and drew in
A breath of river air. A rook's wet wing
Cuffed abruptly upward through the drizzle.

On either hand dead trunks in drapes of creeper,
Strangled softly by horse-mushroom, writhed
In vanished passion, broken down like sponge.
I walked their hushed stations, passion dying,
Each slow footfall a drop of peace returning.

I clapped my gloves. Three cattle turned aside
Their fragrant bodies from a corner gate
And down the sucking chaos of a hedge
Churned land to liquid in their dreamy passage.
Briefly through the beaded grass a path
Led to the holy stillness of a well
And there in the smell of water, stone and leaf
I knelt, baring my hand, and scooped and drank,
Shivering, and inch by inch rejoiced:
Ferocity became intensity.

Or so it seemed as with a lighter step
I turned an ivied corner to confront
The littered fields where summer broke and fled.

Below me, right and left, the valley floor
Tilted in a silence full of storms;
A ruined aqueduct in delicate rigor
Clenched cat-backed, rooted to one horizon;
A vast asylum reared its potent calm
Up from the other through the sodden air,
Tall towers ochre where the gutters dripped;
A steeple; the long yielding of a railway turn
Through thorn and willow; a town endured its place . . .

Joining the two slopes, blocking an ancient way
With crumbled barracks, castle and brewery
It took the running river, wrinkling and pouring
Into its blunt embrace. A line of roofs
Fused in veils of rain and steely light
As the dying sun struck it huge glancing blows.
A strand of idle smoke mounted until
An idler current combed it slowly west,
A hook of shadow dividing the still sky . . .
Mated, like a fall of rock, with time,
The place endured its burden: as a froth
Locked in a swirl of turbulence, a shape
That forms and fructifies and dies, a wisp
That hugs the bridge, an omphalos of scraps.

I moved, my glove-backs glistening, over flesh-
And forest-fed earth; till, skirting a marshy field
Where melancholy brambles scored the mud
By the gapped glitter of a speckled ford,
I shuddered with a visual sweet excitement.

Those murmuring shallows made a trampling place
Apt for death-combat, as the tales agree:
There, the day that Christ hung dying, twin
Brothers armed in hate on either side;
The day darkened but they moved to meet
With crossed swords under a dread eclipse
And mingled their bowels at the saga's end.
There the first Normans massacred my fathers,
Then stroked their armoured horses' necks, disposed
In ceremony, sable on green sward.
Twice more the reeds grew red, the stones obscured;
When knot-necked Cromwell and his fervent sword
Despatched a convent shrieking to their Lover,
And when in peasant fear a rebel host,
Through long retreat grown half hysterical
—Methodical, ludicrous—piked in groups of three
Cromwell's puritan brood, their harmless neighbours,
Forked them half living to the sharp water
And melted into the martyred countryside,
Root eaters, strange as badgers. Pulses calmed;
The racked heroic nerved itself for peace;
Then came harsh winters, motionless waterbirds,
And generations that let welcome fail.

Road and river parted. Now my path
Lay gleaming through the greasy dusk, uphill
Into the final turn. A concrete cross
Low in the ditch grew to the memory
Of one who answered latest the phantom hag,
Tireless Rebellion, when with mouth awry
She hammered at the door, disrupting harvest.
There he bled to death, his line of sight

95

Blocked by the corner-stone, and did not see
His town ablaze with joy, the grinning foe
Driven in heavy lorries from the field;
And he lay cold in the Hill Cemetery
When freedom burned his comrades' itchy palms,
Too much for flesh and blood, and—armed in hate—
Brother met brother in a modern light.
They turned the bloody corner, knelt and killed,
Who gather still at Easter round his grave,
Our watchful elders. Deep in his crumbled heart
He takes their soil, and chatting they return
To take their town again, that have exchanged
A trenchcoat playground for a gombeen jungle.

Around the corner, in an open square,
I came upon the sombre monuments
That bear their names: MacDonagh & McBride,
Merchants; Connolly's Commercial Arms . . .
Their windows gave me back my stolid self
In attitudes of staring as I paced
Their otherworldly gloom, reflected light
Playing on lens and raincoat stonily.
I turned away. Down the sloping square
A lamp switched on above the urinal;
Across the silent handball alley, eyes
That never looked on lover measured mine
Over the Christian Brothers' frosted glass
And turned away. Out of the neighbouring shades
A car plunged soundlessly and disappeared
Pitching downward steeply to the bridge.
I too descended. Naked sycamores,
Gathered dripping near the quay, stood still

And dropped from their combining arms a single
Word upon my upturned face. I trod
The river underfoot; the parapet
Above the central arch received my hands.

Under a darkening and clearing heaven
The hastening river streamed in a slate sheen,
Its face a-swarm. Across the swollen water
(Delicate myriads vanishing in a breath)
Faint ripples winked; a thousand currents broke,
Kissing, dismembering, in threads of foam
Or poured intact over the stony bed
Glass-green and chill; their shallow, shifting world
Slid on in troubled union, forging together
Surfaces that gave and swallowed light;
And grimly the flood divided where it swept
An endless debris through the failing dusk
Under the thudding span beneath my feet.

Venit Hesperus;
In green and golden light; bringing sweet trade.
The inert stirred. Heart and tongue were loosed:
"The waters hurtle through the flooded night . . ."

Downstream

Drifting to meet us on the darkening stage
A pattern shivered; whorling in its place
Another held us in a living cage
Then broke to its reordered phase of grace.

✠

Again in the mirrored dusk the paddles sank.
    We thrust forward, swaying both as one.
    The ripples scattered to the ghostly bank

Where willows, with their shadows half undone,
    Hung to the water, mowing like the blind.
    The current seized our skiff. We let it run

Grazing the reeds, and let the land unwind
    In stealth on either hand. Dark woods: a door
    Opened and shut. The clear sky fell behind,

The channel shrank. Thick slopes from shore to shore
    Lowered a matted arch. I thought of roots
    Crawling full of pike on the river-floor

To cage us in, sensed the furred night-brutes
    Halt in their trails, twitching their tiny brushes.
    What plops in the reeds, stirs between the shoots?

Then I remembered how among those bushes
    A man one night fell sick and left his shell
    Collapsed, half eaten, like a rotted thrush's

To frighten stumbling children. "You could tell,"
    My co-shadow murmured, "by the hands
    He died in terror." And the cold of hell,

A limb-lightness, a terror in the glands,
    Pierced again as when that story first
    Froze my blood: the soil of other lands

Drank lives that summer with a body thirst;
    Nerveless by the European pit
    —Ourselves through seven hundred years accurst—

We saw the barren world obscurely lit
    By tall chimneys flickering in their pall,
    The haunt of swinish man—each day a spit

That, turning, sweated war, each night a fall
    Back to the evil dream where rodents ply,
    Man-rumped, sow-headed, busy with whip and maul,

Among nude heards of the damned. It seemed that I,
    Coming to conscience on that lip of dread,
    Still dreamed, impervious to calamity,

Imagining a formal drift of the dead
    Stretched calm as effigies on velvet dust,
    Scattered on starlit slopes with arms outspread

And eyes of silver—when that story thrust
    Pungent horror and an actual mess
    Into my very face, and taste I must.

Then hungry joy and sickening distress
    Fumbled together by the brimming flood,
    And night consumed a hopeless loneliness.

Like mortal jaws, the alleys of the wood
    Fell-to behind us. At its heart, a ghost
    Glimmered briefly with my gift of blood

—Spreadeagled on a rack of leaves, almost
    Remembering. It looked full at the sky,
    Calmly encountering the starry host,

Meeting their silver eyes with silver eye.
    An X of wavering flesh, a skull of light,
    Extinguished in our wake without a sigh.

Then the current shuddered in its flight
    And swerved on pliant muscle; we were sped
    Through sudden peace into a pit of night:

The Mill-Hole, whose rocky fathoms fed
    On moss and pure depth and the cold fin
    Turning in its heart. The river bed

Called to our flesh. Across the watery skin,
    Breathless, our shell trembled. The abyss . . .
    We shipped our oars in dread. Now, deeper in,

Something shifted in sleep, a quiet hiss
    As we slipped by. Adrift . . . A milk-white breast . . .
    A shuffle of wings betrayed with feathery kiss

A soul of white with darkness for a nest.
    The creature bore the night so tranquilly
    I lifted up my eyes. There without rest

The phantoms of the overhanging sky
    Occupied their stations and descended;
    Another moment, to the starlit eye,

The slow, downstreaming dead, it seemed, were blended
    One with those silver hordes, and briefly shared
    Their order, glittering. And then impended

A barrier of rock that turned and bared
    A varied barrenness as toward its base
    We glided—blotting heaven as it towered—

Searching the darkness for a landing place.

Girl on a Swing

My touch has little force:
Her infant body falls.
Her lips lightly purse
With panic and delight
And fly up to kiss
The years' brimming glass;
To drink; to sag sweetly
When I drop from sight.

A Note About the Author

Thomas Kinsella was born in Dublin in 1928. His first collection, *Poems,* was published in Ireland in 1956, followed by *Another September* in 1958 and *Downstream* in 1962, both the latter being choices of the Poetry Book Society, London. His first collection to be published in this country, *Poems and Translations* (1961), received the Irish Arts Council's Triennial Book Award. A limited edition of the sequence *Wormwood,* included in the present volume, received Ireland's principal recognition for poetry, the Denis Devlin Memorial Award, in 1967. Mr. Kinsella resigned from the Department of Finance in Ireland in 1965 and is at present Professor of English at Southern Illinois University.

A Note on the Type

The text of this book was set on the Linotype in Garamond (No. 3), a modern rendering of the type first cut in the sixteenth century by Claude Garamond (1510–1561). He was a pupil of Geoffroy Troy and is believed to have based his letters on the Venetian models, although he introduced a number of important differences, and it is to him we owe the letter which we know as Old Style. He gave to his letters a certain elegance and a feeling of movement which won for their creator an immediate reputation and the patronage of the French King, Francis I.

This book was composed, printed, and bound by The Kingsport Press, Inc., Kingsport, Tennessee. Typography and binding design by A. Lingeman.